I
WAS
THERE

RICHARD RAVEN

This is a work of nonfiction.

Ordering Information:

Prime Seven Media
518 Landmann St.
Tomah City, WI 54660

Printed in the United States of America

Table of Contents

I was there is not just a story. It came to me over months reading the gospels in the Bible.

As I read these amazing historical records, I could see the events unfolding in my mind's eye. It was as if I really was there.

Next, I wrote it all down, to enable others to experience what I had. Later on, I read the Easter Story out live on Regional Radio and was told the story is inspired. That surprised me, but on consideration, I could see that in fact it is. Plainly, this message is not from me, but a far greater author.

I encourage you to read this short book, and if you can, allow yourself to be there, in the story like I was.

Then I encourage you further to obtain a recent publication of the Bible and read the book of Mark for starters.

If you are like me, from there you will be keen to read it all.

Richard Raven

Shepherds

*I*t is rugged country, beautiful and fresh in spring, when the wild flowers carpet the rocky hill sides, but cold, bleak and wind swept in mid winter. I was there. Out in the pasture with the other sheep men.

Then all at once he was there amongst us. It was weird. He was amazingly radiant, you know, brilliantly incandescent. But the light didn't seem to come only from him, it was all around him. The camp fires that had been so bright before seemed dull and lifeless in this - luminescence. We were all really scared; well anyone would be. There he was all of a sudden in the midst of us.

And his voice, soft but vibrant : a bit like thunder far away, or like a waterfall in the distance, and he said: "Don't be afraid. I am here with good news for you, which will bring great joy to all the people. This very day in David's town our Saviour was born

- Christ the Lord" And he said he could prove it. He said we would find a baby properly wrapped up, in a manger.

Then, all of a sudden, there were thousands and thousands of them, like an enormous army. All glowing like the messenger was. And they were all singing. The noise was terrific! We were terrified at that point, thought our end had come. Then we heard the words of the songs. They were all singing "Glory to God in the highest heaven, and peace on earth to those with whom He is pleased". Then they were all gone! Just gone!

We all talked at once, you know how people are when they have come through something really frightening, or wonderful? Well, we all decided that we just had to go to Bethlehem; right there and then. So off we went, in the middle of the night.

Out there, we always see shooting stars, and other wonderful things, but that one was different. It seemed to hang in space, but keep moving - the weirdest thing I ever saw. One of the men called out when he saw it, and we all turned our attention to this ......light. It wasn't twinkling at all - just steadily shining. In some ways, the star seemed to beckon us, it seemed to move away from us - you know, so slowly, and as it seemed to be going where we were, we followed it.

Sounds pretty stupid, doesn't it? Imagine following the moon, or the sun, and here we were, in the middle of the cold, frosty night, walking after a star! I mean, how ridiculous. And yet, it didn't seem at all silly then, I just knew I had to get nearer to it - didn't know why. I found out later, talking to the others that they were the same. And, you know, even then, in the middle of the night, at one stage, when we were on the top of a hill, I saw a caravan away in the distance. Well, this is the strange part, because, these caravans always carried a good deal of money, and silks and spices and so on. So, they always camped well before sundown, in safe places - usually two or three caravans together.

Yet, here it was almost midnight, and this caravan was travelling. Yes, moving along without any apparent regard for the danger. And as the night was amazingly clear, I could plainly see some men way out front, leading the rest of the caravan. Imagine that, those men striding along, probably following the same star as we were, in the middle of the night.

The star seemed to stop moving when we were just on the outskirts of Bethlehem. We sheep men all came from the neighbouring village, but we knew Bethlehem pretty well. Not much of a town that one. No night life. Nothing like Jerusalem, or any of the big towns up north (that I have heard of) And here we were in the yard of the crummy Bethlehem Inn. What a joint. Not big enough to put up more than about ten people, let alone their servants and animals.

By the time we got there, it was really late, and we were tired, so we went to the stables to see if there was room for us to bed down. Well, being sheep men, we never could afford to pay for a room, or even to sleep in the main hall near the fire. I tried to get a bed in an inn once, but the landlord must have had something wrong with his nose, kept sniffing and complaining; he said I smelled! So we always just slept in the stables - on clean straw - it was still better than outside in the cold.

Well, this is the amazing part. When we got there, in the stables, there was already a young couple there. And she had had a baby! Just imagine having a baby there in the stables, with a soft eyed cow quietly chewing, and making sort of contented noises, and a few donkeys just standing in their stalls, breathing steamy breath. There was a pair of doves in the rafters quietly murmuring to each other, and, well it is hard to put into words, but the whole picture is as bright in my mind now as I tell you, as if it was happening now.

The incredible thing wasn't really any of the things I have told you, it was the baby. I have never seen a baby like him. He was different. There seemed to be ....light all around him. Oh, his mother was beautiful, radiant, you know, but this light was round the baby! Like the light out there in the pasture, but this time the light was right round that beautiful little bundle. And the atmosphere there. The feeling there in those stables was the most peaceful I had ever known.

We seemed to be there just minutes, but, next thing, it was daylight, and we knew we had to get back to our sheep. On the way out of Bethlehem, the caravan we had seen far away from the hill came into the yard, with a small group of men leading the way. They were probably the same men we had seen the night before. Funny looking blokes - you know? Like magicians, or professors or something. They were certainly not sheep men I can tell you that. They so much intrigued me, that I told my friends that I had to go back to the stables for something, and I would catch up to them later.

When I got back there, these magicians, or astrologers, or whatever they were, were unpacking some sort of parcels, and giving them to the little baby.

Well they said they were for the baby, but gave them to the Father. I suppose he was the father, why else would he be there, obviously very attached to the Mother.

And you know what these men were giving this baby, lying there in the stables of this crummy little inn?

One of them gave gold jewellery. I know real gold when I see it, it was plainly heavy, and gleamed, you know like gold. The second man gave him frankincense. And the third man gave him myrrh! This baby was obviously special. His own star, his own angels and his own magicians and these fabulous presents. Then I heard one of the magicians say that on the way, they had spoken to King Herod. They told the Father and Mother that they didn't trust Herod, and they were going home the long way to make sure he wouldn't interfere with them.

I stayed another day, I was just fascinated really. I tell you, there was something about that baby. He really was special.

In the morning, the Father said they were going to another town. I had met him by then - his name was Joseph. He was a bit strange really. We all know God gives us our new lambs, and even our own little children, but this Joseph said that Mary's baby (that is his wife's baby) was God's child. I suppose he was just excited about the new babe, and being a Father, and everything.

So, after a little while, they packed up the baby, (his name was Jesus) and the gold and the frankincense and the myrrh, and Mary got on their little donkey with everything, and they left. Well, I went back to the sheep. But I knew I had been changed somehow by the events of that night.

Purification

My family is very large. It is surprising really, since so many of my Uncles never married. One of these uncles was named Simeon, and at the time Joseph and Mary went to the Temple, he was there. Well, that is also not surprising, because he went there almost every day.

He always had said that God would not allow him to die until he had seen our Messiah; and he was a very holy man. He was very very old, I don't know how old, but I know he didn't have many teeth, and his face was so wrinkled and creased. He was nearly deaf and his sight was very bad, but it always amazed me how bright his eyes were. They seemed to twinkle and somehow even though he couldn't see well, the light seemed to come from his eyes.

They all said he was filled with the spirit of God like old Anna the prophetess who also seemed to be at the Temple all the time. Some one told me she was so old, she had been a widow for eighty four years! She must have been over one hundred years old. She really looked it too.

I suppose the best thing about going from job to job is the variety of people you meet, and the experience of learning different jobs.

That is how it has always been with me. I spent years working as a sheep man, and a farm worker, a wine maker's assistant, harvest hand, fruit picker, and even worked on the Roman roads for a while.

That is how I came to see that wonderful little boy again: the one who was born in the stables.

I was in Jerusalem one Sabbath. After Joseph, Mary and little Jesus had left Bethlehem, they must have kept moving, but they went up to Jerusalem for the required purification ceremony. Following our custom, Mary was considered unclean for forty days after childbirth (it would have been twice as long if she had had a girl) and she wouldn't be permitted to go into the Temple until the Priest had performed the ritual cleansing.

So, on the forty first day after Jesus was born, Joseph and Mary went to the Temple at Jerusalem where they needed to offer the sacrifices: one dove as a burnt offering, and one as the sin offering.

So then my Uncle Simeon took baby Jesus in his arms, and started proclaiming in a loud voice. He said "This child has a wonderful destiny. He will cause some to fall and others to rise. As a result, the very deepest thought of many will be revealed, and a sword will pierce you to your very soul" Wow! What did all this mean?

Then Anna, the old lady came up and began praising God. She said to Mary and Joseph, "This child is the one we all had been waiting for. He has been sent to rescue Israel" Wow again!

I was there in the temple on another Passover day, it was probably twelve years later. Jesus and his parents were there. You should have seen this little man then. Not just a twelve year old. Oh no! He had a presence about him, a confidence. Way out of my league I can tell you.

Well, after the ceremonies were concluded, the wave of people were leaving. All going back to the town, villages, and even countries from where they came. But there was a mix-up or something because, that night, Joseph and Mary found Jesus was not with them. Where could he be?

I tagged along as they returned to the Temple, you know, to see if I could be of help or something. I really do not know why I was there, but I was. And when they entered the Temple, there was young Jesus. In the midst of all the Priests, and other smart people, asking questions of them, and answering their questions. You would think he was a Priest too, or something.

When Mary said "Why did you not come with us Son, we were worried" But, Jesus said the most amazing thing. He said "Surely you would know I would be in my Father's house. Where else"?

The First Disciples and First Miracle

One day, I had been attracted to the spectacle of that wild man John who was dunking people in the Jordan River, He told them to repent, and turn back to God. He had been doing this for several days, and naturally, had attracted a large following. This particular day, as I had no work, I was there too, along with very many similarly unemployed folks. Then I saw Jesus coming to John. This surprised me, as I had not seen him since he was a twelve year old boy. He was now and upright man, of some thirty odd years, with the look of quiet confidence about him, the look that I would later understand as purpose. He really knew beyond doubt, his place in the world.

On this day, as he walked towards John the Baptizer, as he was called, John, who was a cousin of some sort, said to his followers " Look. Here he is, the Lamb of God. He takes away the sin of the world" Jesus asked to be baptized, and after John demurring, he eventually was. On coming up out of the water, John said "I see the Spirit of God appearing like a dove, and landing on Him. God had told me I would baptize the one who would baptize with the Holy Spirit, and this is he. The Son of God"

On hearing this, two of Johns followers, left him, and started following Jesus. Who looked around and asked them why the followed him. One of them, said "Teacher, where are you living?" Jesus said "Come and see for yourselves" Why would anyone follow someone as enigmatic as that? I do not know, but I too tagged along behind them.

One of these two was named Andrew, and he went to his brother Simon and told him "we have found the anointed one, or in Jewish terms the Messiah" Then when Andrew brought Simon to Jesus, Jesus said to him "Yes, you are Simon, son of John, but from now on you will be called Cephas" This means Stone, or rock. That mystified me, but I was to hear and see many more amazing things over the coming months and years. The next day, on the way to Gallillee, Jesus came to Philip, and told him to come and follow him. Incredibly, Philip then went to find his friend Nathanael, and told him "We have found the one we have been waiting for. He is Jesus from Nazareth. The one Moses and the Prophets foretold" But Nathanael, curled his lip, and said "What good thing ever came from Nazareth?" But Philip just said "Come and let's find out" Now the amazing part of this story, is when Nathanael came toward Jesus, He said, "Here comes a true Son of Israel. An honest man with no hidden agenda" But Nathanael was surprised by this statement, and said "But we have never met. How can you know anything about me?" Jesus replied " Nathanael, I saw you when you sat under the shade of that fig tree" This blew Nathanael away, and he gushed "Teacher, you really are the Son of God and the King of Israel"

The thing about weddings at the time Jesus lived, is that after the two families had arranged all the details, the couple would be betrothed. Their betrothal would last some months, often an entire year. Then the two families would get together, inviting every possible important person connected not just to the families, but in the towns involved. The numbers were very difficult to predict, as many people were invited to swell the numbers, and to cover the fact that many folk just do not turn up. These were really grand affairs for those who could afford the expense. Naturally, some competition was seen to have each wedding more lavish that the last in the village. The cost of these weddings was huge, involving great quantities of food and wine.

Mary, Jesus and his brothers and sisters were invited to such a wedding at a town called Cana, and most of Jesus' followers were there too. With all my cousins, I am connected with some of the families involved, so I was there too. Certainly not as an important person, and I think I attended quite unobtrusively.

There were very many people there, in fact, many more than had been expected. Because of this, the food ran short, making those responsible for cooking to keep slaving in the cook house, but worse than that, the wine had almost run out. What an embarrassment for the hosts, as even though they could have had little idea how many were to attend, it was their responsibility to ensue no-one went away hungry are with unslaked thirst.

Well, you know, weddings with all the talking , singing and dancing are thirsty events.

You just cannot run out of wine. That is the unwritten law of hospitality where we live.

Mary came up to Jesus, who was not far from where I was standing, and said "They are running out of wine. Can you do something about it?" That surprised me, because as guests ourselves, we had no responsibility to provide. Jesus, as calm as I ever saw him said "Mother Dear, I understand your desires, but my time has not yet come" But Mary simply went to the servers, and told them to do whatever Jesus said. What on earth did she mean?

There were several large pots there for water needed for ceremonious washing before a meal. Jesus told the servers to fill these pots to the brim with water. Then he said "Fill your pitchers from the pots, and take them to the Master of Ceremonies" What was happening here? You just cannot take water to the MC and pretend it is wine.

But they did exactly that. As mere servants it was not their problem.

Then I waited for the uproar when the unimaginable happened. They poured from the pitchers into the MC goblet, and he tasted it. Here we go I thought.

But I was wrong. As wrong as I could ever be. Because, the MC smiled enormously, and declared this the best wine he had ever tasted. And it was. I had some too. Jesus had turned ordinary well water into the finest red wine. How?

Miracles/
Seven loaves/
The Christ

After some time, Jesus and all his followers went from Galilee up to Tyre He tried to keep his presence a secret, but that didn't last long. For a start, there was all of us, his followers, people he had cured, people who just worshipped him, people intrigued by his mere presence, people just there to enjoy the show. How could anyone ever keep it quiet that Jesus of Nazareth was in a town, even a place as big as Tyre?

No sooner than we had established ourselves there, than a woman brought her little girl, who she said was possessed by a demon. Any one could see this child was possessed, much as I had seen others; screaming, face contorted, convulsing, throwing herself on the ground and then leaping up again. Then becoming as nice as any little child, smiling so sweetly, and timidly coming up to you and taking your hand; then biting your hand and bringing blood. She was possessed all right! But we could not understand why this woman was asking our Master for his assistance - she was Syrophoenician; a gentile!

We all expected the Master to send her away; oh he would have done it nicely, but we knew he would send her away. So when he said to her "First, I should help my own family, my Jewish brothers and sisters. It isn't right to take the childrens' food and throw it to the dogs" We all knew exactly what he said, we all called gentiles dogs ourselves. What a brilliant man Jesus was, sending this woman away without really saying "no" showing her that she shouldn't have asked him at all.

But, typical of those people, who never take "no" for an answer, this stupid woman tried to match wits with our Master. She said " That's true sir, but even the puppies under the table are given some scraps from the childrens' plates." She was pretty clever herself, and we just waited to see how Jesus put her in her place. How would he do it?

He said "Good, you have answered well. So well, that I have healed your little girl. Take her home now, for the demon has left her" One thing we all agreed on, was the Master's unpredictable way with people. He was stern with important people, and soft with this gentile woman. Just when we expected him to simply say "Go away woman, I am here for the Jews"- and he just said "You have answered well. So I have healed your little girl"

And he had healed her. I don't know what happens to demons when they are cast out, but this child was different. She had a different light in her eyes. She looked happier, and healthier. It was obvious she was cured.

After a time in Tyre, Jesus went to Sidon, and of course, we all followed him.

Everywhere we went, Jesus healed people. He healed them from minor ailments, and sometimes very major illness.

Sometimes, he cured deformity, and disfigurement that people had suffered all their lives.

One such man was brought to Jesus after we had returned via the Decapolis (that is the group of ten towns) to the sea of Galilee. This man was deaf and dumb; well he could talk, but not very well, and many people could never understand what he said. He had been like this all his life.

The people who brought him were his brothers, and they begged Jesus to cure him of his affliction.

Jesus lead this man away from the crowd, and put his fingers into the man's ears. Then he pulled them out, and spat on his fingers, and touched the man's tongue with the spittle. Then he looked up to heaven, sighed and he said clearly "Open"

You should have seen the look on the man's face. He could hear ! He started to shout, then realised he could speak properly ! The look on his face was absolutely wonderful. Sort of fear, and adoration and joy and everything all moving over his face at once. Jesus told the crowd not to tell anyone about these cures, but of course, the more he said "Do not speak of this", the more every one did speak of his healings. He must have known they would; he knew every thing else.

There was another day, when the crowd of followers and local people was enormous. There must have been at least 4000 people there, all trying to be in the front, to see better, to hear every word that Jesus spoke. We had all been there almost three days, and I doubt anyone brought enough food for that time. I heard some of the children complaining they were hungry. I was too, and I suppose many people were, but there was nothing to eat out there.

I was at the front of the crowd, where I usually maneuvered myself, and I heard Jesus say to one of his disciples "I pity these people. They have nothing left to eat. If I send them home without feeding them, some of them will faint on the way". His disciple thought this was some sort of joke, as he said "Are we supposed to find food out here in the desert?" Jesus asked him "How much bread do we have left?" and the answer was seven loaves.

Jesus asked the crowd to sit down, then he took the seven loaves and a few small fish that some one had there, thanked God for this food, broke them, and had his disciples pass this food around the crowd. This huge crowd ate for ages, and everyone seemed to have quite enough. After they had all gone, the disciples collected seven large baskets full of the leftovers !

A few days later, we all had gone to Caesarea Philippi, north of the Sea of Galilee, and walking along, Jesus asked his disciples, "Who are the people saying I am?"

Different ones said different things, all trying to please him, I suppose.

One said "John the Baptist" another said "Elijah", someone else said "One of the prophets that has been brought back to life"

Then He said "Who do you think I am?" They had already given their answers. Each turned to the other, as if to ask the same question. But not so Simon Peter, the big man. He looked straight at Jesus, with a look almost of wonder on his big benevolent face. He looked a little surprised at the words coming out of his own mouth - as if they were not really his words. He said "You are the Christ, the Messiah, the Son of the Living God."

We were all struck dumb. What a thing to say. Who would have thought of it?

Jesus just looked at Simon Peter for a moment, then He said "God has blessed you Simon, son of Jonah, for my Father in heaven has personally revealed this to you. This thought is not of any human source."

We all stared at Peter then. Peter, the big man had received a message directly from God! Then Jesus said " You are Peter, a stone, and upon this rock I will build my church; and all the powers of the evil one shall never prevail against it." Then He said "I ask you to keep this to yourselves. This is our secret now. The time will come for you to tell the whole world what you know of me, but that time is not now. I will tell you when that time has come."

Then he began telling all who could hear Him, all the terrible things that were to happen to Him. None of us could stand to hear these things, the false accusation and trial of our Lord, the future King of Israel, and his crucifixion and death. That great big soft Peter, couldn't stand it, and was also concerned that some of the followers may misunderstand all this talk of suffering and dying, and drift away. So he took Jesus by the elbow, and said to Him "You shouldn't say these horrible things, Master"

Jesus turned, looked at His disciples, then looked straight at Peter, and said in the sternest voice "Satan - get behind me!" Then in his usual teaching tone of voice, he said "Peter, you do not understand yet, and are looking at this from the human perspective, but I only see it from God's perspective." Then he called together all of us who followed Him everywhere, and said "If any of you would follow me, you must put aside your own pleasures, shoulder your cross, and follow me closely. If you insist on saving your life, you will lose it. Only those who throw away their own lives for my sake, and the sake of the Good News will ever know what it means to really live.

We all found this very difficult to understand, and He was saying more. He said "And how does a man benefit, if he gains the whole world, but loses his soul in the process ? For is anything worth more than his soul? And anyone who is ashamed of me and my message, in these days of unbelief, and sin, I, the Messiah will be ashamed of him, when I return to the Glory of my Father, with the holy angels. But, this is the simple truth - some of you who are standing here right now, will not die, until you have seen the Kingdom of God."

The Mighty Miracle

Some rich people travel in chariots, usually Romans. Some of us Jews travel on a donkey, but for most of us, we walk. We walk everywhere. So it was that Jesus and all his followers, and there were very many of them by now, walked all the way from the Mount of Olives, just out of Jerusalem, to the Jordan River, very close to the place where I had seen Jesus baptized by John the Baptizer. That was quite a journey, with people along the way asking for healing, and blessings of all sorts. Someone told me at some stage that we walked something like eight thousand paces every day. No wonder I was tired! But Jesus seemed tireless, and just kept moving for days. So it was that we took two days to reach the Jordan River. The spot where we camped was just over the other side, so we had to wade through the shallows to get there. At least that was cool on our feet!

We had been there only a short time, when a messenger arrived from Bethany where Jesus' friends Martha and Mary lived with their brother Lazarus. I am not close enough to Jesus to know why, but he really loved these three. I do know that the girls helped Jesus with money and supplies at times, as good friends do.

The messenger told Jesus that Lazarus was really sick and in a bad way. I do know there was great concern in the messenger for his master Lazarus, who was a really good man. But Jesus was unconcerned about the report of his friend's health. He said "Do not concern yourself. This sickness will not cause Lazarus to die. No, God will receive Glory because of his sickness."

We all talked amongst ourselves as to how he became sick. Who had sinned, who had broken God's laws and so on, because it was known that sinning caused death. Jesus heard us, as he seemed to always hear us, and explained that sickness does not indicate that God has rejected someone. Rather, we all become sick from time to time, as a part of living. So we stayed there beside the Jordan for two more days.

On the morning of the third day, Jesus said " Let us go back to Judea" which was the west side of the river. Some of his close followers thought that would be dangerous, as only a few days earlier, the Jews there tried to kill him. But Jesus said "Are there not twelve hours of daylight? If people walk in the light, they will not stumble, but if they walk in the dark anything could happen"

I couldn't follow half of the things he said, and this was no different. Walking in the light or the dark. How senseless is that? Then Jesus said "Our friend Lazarus has fallen asleep. I will wake him up" Nobody understood and someone said "Lord, if he is just asleep, he will wake up himself" But Jesus said "Lazarus is dead. For your benefit it is good we were not there. Now you will see and believe."

By the time we arrived back at Bethany, where the family lived, Lazarus had been dead and buried four days ago. Martha came out to meet Jesus, and said "Lord, if you had been here our brother Lazarus would not have died. Jesus simply said "Martha, your brother will rise again" Martha said she thought Jesus meant that all believers would rise on the last day, but Jesus said " I am the resurrection and the Life. Whoever believes in me will live, even if they die. Whoever lives in me by believing in me will never die. Do you believe this?"

Martha said "Yes Lord. I believe you are the Messiah, the Son of God that the scriptures foretold."

Martha then went back to the house, the house full of mourning, and told Mary that Jesus was where she had met him. Mary immediately got up, and rushed to that place. When she saw him, she fell at his feet and said "Lord, if you had been here, our brother would not have died." Such was their faith in Jesus' healing powers.

Several of the Jews and other mourners who had been at the house had followed Mary, and noticed how emotional Jesus had become. They thought because of the death of his friend. Someone said "He cured blindness, surely he could have kept this man from death"

As they approached the cave where Lazarus had been laid, Jesus said "Take away the stone." Because as is usual, a large stone had been rolled over the cave entrance to keep animals out. But Martha said "But Lord, he has been dead four days and will smell terribly"

Jesus said "Remember I said you will see God's Glory?" So they took away the stone, and Jesus callout in a loud voice "Lazarus, come out" All of us there were shocked. Calling to a dead man to come out of his tomb! But he did!

Lazarus, wrapped in his burial cloths walked with difficulty, but he walked out of his tomb! I saw this! He walked unaided. He was not dead any more. There was no stink! He walked!

Jesus said "Take off his burial cloths, and let him go."

Nobody spoke.

Palm Sunday

After meeting Jesus of Nazareth, many people just left what they were doing, and followed Him. Fishermen were known to just leave their boats and nets on the beach, and walk off. He had that effect on people. He had that effect on me, and after He cured me, well, I wanted to be with Him, and like so many others, I followed Him. Oh, He would slip away at times, but we soon found where He was, and we went there. While He had some special friends, none of the rest of us was ever pushed away.

So it was that I was often close by Him, and one such time was when He was preparing to go to Jerusalem for the Passover which would be in six days time. He and some special friends had been staying at Bethany, at the home of Lazarus, the man who died, and Jesus had brought him back to life. On the way to Jerusalem, they were all talking about the waste of perfume and money. Mary had anointed Jesus feet with Nard. That is so expensive only Kings get to have it and then usually after they die. From what was said, the amount Mary used would cost more than I could ever earn in a year. And they were talking about Jesus' answer when Judas Iscariot questioned Mary's values. Jesus had said, "Let her alone, she did it in preparation for my burial. You can always help the poor, but (he said) I won't be with you very long" Naturally, none of us understood what He meant.

You should have seen the mobs waiting when we arrived at Jerusalem. Word had spread that Jesus was arriving, and also that the Man who had been dead was with Him. Many people had palm branches which they spread out on the dusty road, and people everywhere were chanting Jesus' name. Others were calling out "The Saviour" and "God bless the King of Israel" and others "Hail to God's Ambassador" It was a great reception, with much excitement, and there was Jesus on that little donkey. He didn't look much like a King really, and yet, he just had that aura, that presence - I've never known any one else like Him.

He certainly had that presence when he strode into the court of the gentiles in the temple, and when he drove the merchants out, and overturned the money changers' tables and let the animals loose. He had that magnificent presence, and absolute authority, when he stood in the centre of the court yard, and addressing the Priests, said "The scriptures say my temple is a house of prayer, but you have turned it into a den of thieves"

And then the blind and cripples came to Him, and he healed them all. The children were shouting, "God bless the Son of David" The priests said to him "Do you hear what they are saying?" and Jesus replied "Yes, didn't you ever read the scriptures ? For they say 'Even the little babies will praise Him!' " Then He went back to Bethany, where He stayed the night. That was to be His pattern for the rest of the week; staying at Bethany every night, and teaching in the Temple every day.

One morning, as we were all going back to Jerusalem, Jesus was hungry, and He went up to a fig tree growing on the side of the road. But there was not even one fig on the tree, just leaves. Jesus said to the tree "Never bear fruit again" It seemed a bit strange to speak to a tree like that, but we were all amazed to see almost immediately, that the tree just withered up from the roots. It was dead!

Someone said to Him "How did that happen?" Jesus replied " Truly, if you have faith, and don't doubt, you can do things like this, and much more. You can even say to this Mount of Olives "Move into the ocean" and it will. You can get anything - anything that you ask for in prayer....if you believe"

A little later, after we had gone back to the Temple, the chief priests and other leaders come up to Jesus, and were really agitated. One of them demanded of Him "What's going on? Who gave you authority to drive out the merchants?"

Jesus just turned His marvelous eyes on the priest, and said so calmly "I'll tell you if you answer one question. What about John the Baptist? Was he sent by God, or not? Answer me!"

Well, you should have seen the priests right then, they went all furtive, and muttered amongst themselves, and seemed to get really bad tempered. One of them said "We can't win this, we never accepted that John came from God, yet the people will start a riot if we say so" And then the chief priest said "We can't answer, we don't know"

Jesus simply said "Then I won't answer your question either"

He had won, he had beaten them and made them look foolish in front of all those people, but Jesus seemed hurt right then. Their response seemed to sadden Him.

But He came out of that almost instantly, and started answering questions from the people, teaching them about scripture, and how to live. Some of the questions were legitimate, but we could see that some of them were staged by the priests, trying to catch Him out, but they never could. He just knew their every thought.

Then one of the teachers of religion asked "Of all the commandments, which is the most important?" Here was a test, asking Jesus to evaluate Moses law, the law of all Jews.

But Jesus' answer came almost immediately "The one that says 'Hear O Israel! The Lord our God is the one and only God, and you must love Him with all your heart, and mind and strength.' The second is 'You must love others as much as you love yourself' No other commandments are greater than these "

The teacher was very impressed, we could see that. He said he agreed exactly with Jesus' statement; - and Jesus looked at him for a brief moment, then said "You are not far from the Kingdom of God"

Then the two of them just seemed to read each others eyes and it seemed time stood still. No questions were asked for hours, and Jesus taught all who would hear Him, as He told His stories. The stories that made Scripture live.

Later that day, as we left the temple someone said "what a wonderful building. What beautiful stone work." Jesus replied "Yes look, for not one stone will be left standing on another, all will be in ruins."

Later, as we all sat in a grove on the Mount of Olives, Jesus talked about the terrible time when the world would end, with wars and earthquakes and much much more: that the sun would grow dim, and the moon will stop shining, and the stars will fall. He said that many people would then turn to false messiahs in the terror and confusion. But He said "then all Mankind will see me, coming in the clouds with great power and glory, and I shall send forth my angels with the sound of a mighty trumpet blast and they shall gather my chosen ones from the farthest ends of heaven and earth. My return will not be announced, and no one will know just when I am coming, but there will be signs for those who are watchful. So, as you see these things start to happen, you will know that my return is near. Be ready my friends, because then at last this age will come to a close. Heaven and earth will disappear, but my words will remain for ever."

"The world will be at ease, with parties and festivals and ceremonies, just as it was in Noah's time. People then wouldn't believe there was going to be a flood, until the waters rushed in and they were all taken away. This is how my return shall be, so be prepared, for you don't know what day your Lord is coming."

The Last Supper

Finally, the day for the Passover Celebration arrived, when the Passover Lamb was killed and eaten with the unleavened bread. Jesus sent Peter and John back to Jerusalem to find a place to prepare their Passover meal. He said to them "As soon as you enter Jerusalem, you will find a man carrying a pitcher of water. Follow him to the house he enters, and say to the man who lives there 'Our teacher asks that you show us the guest room, where He can eat the Passover meal with His disciples.'He will take you upstairs to a room all ready for us" They went, and found the man carrying water, even though that is always done by women, and they followed him, and they found the room exactly as Jesus had said.

Then Jesus and we others arrived, and at the proper time, sat down at the table. And Jesus looked around the room at all the people there. He looked at every one of us. He looked at me: and no one spoke. Then He smiled that warm, loving smile that won us all to Him when first we met, and He got up from the table, took off His outer robe, wrapped a towel round his waist like a servant, and poured water into a basin.

Then He started washing the feet of everyone in the room. Jesus, our Lord, our Master was washing our feet! When he came to Simon Peter, Peter said to Him "Master, you shouldn't be washing our feet like this." Jesus replied "You don't understand now why I am doing it; someday you will." But Peter said "No Lord, you shall never wash my feet!" But Jesus answered "If I don't, you can never become my partner." We could see the effect these words had on Peter, who we all admired, and he fell to his knees and said "Then wash my hands and my head as well, not just my feet."

Jesus response was like so many of His sayings , they needed to be thought about by us. He said " One who has bathed all over needs only to have his feet washed to be entirely clean.

Now you are clean - but that isn't true of everyone here."

Then when he had washed everyone's feet he put His robe on again, and sat at the table and said "I have looked forward to this hour with deep longing, anxious to eat this Passover meal with you before my suffering begins. For I tell you now, that I won't eat it again until what it represents has occurred in the Kingdom of God."

Then He took the first of the four ritual glasses of wine, and when He had given thanks for it, He said "Take this and share it amongst yourselves, for I will not drink wine again until the Kingdom of God has come."

Then He took a loaf of bread, and when He had given thanks for it, He broke it apart and handed it to all of us saying "Think of this as my body given for you. Every time you eat it, think of me."

After Supper, Jesus handed out the ceremonial fourth glass of wine and said " Think of this wine as the token of God's New Agreement to save you - an agreement sealed with the blood I shall pour out to purchase back your souls. But here amongst us, sitting at this table as a friend, is the one who will betray me.

I must die, it is part of God's plan. But, oh the horror awaiting the man who betrays me."

Well, you can imagine how we all felt then. Here was our Lord, the King of Israel, talking about being betrayed and of dying. We were all confused, and some started saying "Is it me Lord?" and others were arguing who would have the highest rank in the new kingdom.

Jesus said "A little while ago, I washed your feet. Now I will tell you why. In the outside world, the masters are served by their servants. But not in my world. Among you, the one who serves you best will be your leader. For I am your servant. That is why I washed your feet. Even so, because you have all been true to me, and because my Father has given me a kingdom, I now grant each of you the right to eat and drink at my table in that kingdom, and you will sit on thrones, judging the twelve tribes of Israel."

Now we were confused, because this talk of kingdoms was what we had thought we would hear. But still, the thought of being with Jesus, and helping Him rule was enough for us.

Then Jesus said "Simon Peter, my friend, Satan has asked to have you. But I have asked my Father to uphold you, so you will not fail me completely. So when you have repented, and turned to me again, strengthen and build up the faith of your brothers"

We could see that Peter was moved by this , and we knew he was devoted to Jesus (as we all were) And Peter said "Lord I am ready to go to jail with you, or even to die with you."

Jesus looked lovingly at Peter, and said "Simon, Simon, let me tell you something. Between now and tomorrow morning, before the rooster crows you will deny me three times, declaring that you don't even know me."

Trials

*J*ust moments after Peter had left, I heard some noise inside the house, and moved so I could see into the room. The whole Sanhedrin was assembled there; the entire Supreme Court! Even at this hour in the morning. Then I heard them all shout "Then you claim you are the son of God!"

"Yes." Jesus said " I am" Then the priests went wild. What more do we want? someone yelled, we have all heard Him utter this blasphemy! And they shouted Death! Death! Death! and they hit Him and spat on Him. Then they chained Him, and the entire council took Jesus over to Pilate, the Roman Governor. Pilate knew the Priests couldn't go into his palace the day before the Passover, so he came out to his porch way.

Pilate demanded of the priests "What reason have you brought this man before me in chains?" The priests replied that Jesus had been inciting Jews not to pay Roman taxes, and that He is their Messiah - their King. Pilate turned to Jesus, and demanded "You are the King of the Jews - the Messiah?"

Jesus calmly said " It is as you say." Pilate turned again to the priests, and said "So? That isn't a crime." This seemed to disturb the priests, and one said "But He is causing riots everywhere He goes. All over Judea, from Galilee to Jerusalem."

Pilate seemed to clutch at this statement, and said "Is He Galilean ?"

When they told him that Jesus was, Pilate seemed relieved, and told them to take Jesus to Herod, as Galilee was under Herod's jurisdiction.

So the priests and their mob took Jesus away in chains to Herod, and still I was there. Still I did nothing but watch.

Herod asked question after question, but Jesus made no reply. Herod's soldiers ridiculed Jesus, putting a kingly robe on Him, and finally, they sent Him back to Pilate having gained nothing.

Pilate demanded of Jesus "What have you to say about the priests accusations?" but Jesus said nothing. Normally, when prisoners were accused of any crime, they groveled and whined, or were truculent and aggressive, so Pilate was obviously disturbed by Jesus' serenity and His obvious lack of fear.

Then he called together the chief priests before us and said "I have found no crime against Rome proven against this man. If you have found Him at fault, you take Him and try Him yourselves."

The priests became agitated again at that, and screamed out "But we want Him crucified - your approval is required"

Pilate had been a most unpopular Governor, and there was rumour that he was likely to be removed from his post if there was further trouble in Jerusalem. Only a few days ago, a bandit named Barabbas had been creating disturbances and had been arrested by the Romans for murder. Pilate had for some time been attempting to achieve goodwill from the Jewish leaders, so we were not surprised when Pilate then called Jesus for further questioning.

Again, out on the porch, Pilate said to Jesus "You say you are a King, why do you not say something about the priests' charges?" But Jesus said nothing.

Pilate was clearly uncomfortable about the situation. Again he called the priests together, this time to announced his verdict.

"You brought this man before me, accused Him of leading a revolt against the Roman government. I have examined Him thoroughly on this point, and found Him innocent. Herod came to the same conclusion, and sent Him back to us. He has done nothing to warrant the death penalty. I will therefore have Him scourged , and will release Him."

The mob then screamed for Jesus death. They demanded the release of the bandit Barabbas instead. Pilate argued with them, that Jesus was not guilty of any crime, but Barabbas was a proven murderer. But they would not have Jesus, they shouted "Crucify Him, Crucify Him. Once more, Pilate demanded "What for, what crime has he committed? I have found no reason to sentence Him to death. But they shouted louder and louder for Jesus death. It looked like a riot was forming.

Pilate then called for a bowl of water, and washing his hands in it said "I am washing my hands of the blood of this good man. His death is your responsibility." They shouted back " His blood be on us and our children."

Pilate then had Jesus whipped with the cruel flagellum, which had thongs braided with lead pellets and pieces of bone. It was designed to inflict maximum pain on all those suffering its vicious use, and in a few jarring strikes, Jesus back was laid open. The soldiers then roughly placed a hideous crown of long thorns on His head. Pilate then gave our Lord over to them to be crucified.

I couldn't do anything. I could hardly see through my tears.

Resurrection

The day after the Sabbath is often a busy day, but this Sunday it was really quiet. People were seen speaking in hushed tones. The talk of all Jerusalem was the crucifixion on Friday, and the earthquake and darkness as Jesus died. But more than these, was the talk that right at the time of the earthquake, the curtain in the Temple separating the Holy of Holies from the people was torn from top to bottom. It was 15 metres high!

Who could have torn it but God ? What did it mean ?

The rest of the talk was about a member of the Supreme Court. A man from Arimathea by name of Joseph. He had recently paid workers to dig a tomb intending it for his eventual use. It had a very large stone carved to seal the entrance. He had been given permission by Pilate and had taken Jesus' body down from the Cross. He had wrapped the body in burial clothes, and laid my Jesus in this tomb. The Chief Priest had insisted that the tomb was sealed with the stone and a rope had been fixed to the entrance with sealing clay to stop anyone going in or coming out. And to make sure of it, temple police were posted to guard the entrance.

I don't know what they were afraid of, Jesus was dead.

I was there when Jesus died on the cross. My Jesus was dead. I was there when they took his body down and placed it in that tomb. My Jesus was dead. The life had gone out of me when my Jesus died. I was lost, alone........................ My Jesus was dead.

Early this Sunday I was back in my old job, tidying the gardens near the tombs. Then I saw Mary Magdalene and Salome and Mary the Mother of James walking just ahead of me. They were carrying small pottery flasks like those used for perfumes and oils.

Then they stopped, obviously shocked, and I could see that the great stone sealing the grave was rolled back. The tomb was open! The police were unconscious on the ground.

The women went in, and I moved so as to see what they were doing.

Inside, there was a young man clothed in brilliant white - he was radiant, like the man

I had seen when I was a shepherd some thirty years ago! He said to the women

"Don't be so surprised. Aren't you looking for Jesus, the Nazarene who was crucified?"

They all just stared at him, and he said "He isn't here, He has come back to life! Look, that's where His body was lying. Now go and give this message to His disciples, including Peter: "Jesus is going ahead of you to Galilee. You will see Him there, just as He told you before He died.""

The women just turned and fled from the tomb. They were terrified. When I looked back into the tomb it was empty except for a small pile of grave clothes and the cloth used as a head covering. The young man in shining white was gone!

I just stayed there, I had nowhere to go, I felt lost.

The next thing I remember was Peter and John running up the path towards me, then straight past me as they went into the empty tomb.

Just moments later, they came out again and walked slowly back the way they had come, this time speaking in hushed tones, although John seemed excited about something.

Then Mary came back and again went into the tomb. She was crying. A little later she came out again and seemed surprised to see a man standing there. I hadn't seen him either. I don't know how long he had been there. Thinking that Mary was not in any condition to deal with strangers, I went forward - I don't really know why, I thought she may need me.

He said to her "Why are you crying? Whom are you looking for?"

She said "Sir, if you have taken Him away, tell me where you have put Him, and I will go and get Him."

His voice rang with compassion, and I was stirred from my grief "Mary" he said.

I knew that voice ! I loved that voice ! So did Mary ......"Master" was all she said.

"Don't touch me" He said "I haven't yet ascended to the Father. But go find my brothers, and tell them that I ascend to my Father and your Father, my God and your God. Tell them I will see them in Galilee just like I promised. Tell them you have seen me. They can believe in me and everything I promised."

Then He was gone. Mary stood there for a brief moment, then turned and ran back up the path.

I just stood there. I was trembling all over. I had seen Him. I had heard Him speak.

My Jesus is alive! My Jesus is alive! My Jesus is alive!